Lists!

A Year of Stuff About Me

illustrated by
Julia Bereciartu

Published by American Girl Publishing
Copyright © 2011 by American Girl

Questions or comments? Call 1-800-845-0005,
visit **americangirl.com**, or write to Customer Service,
American Girl, 8400 Fairway Place, Middleton, WI 53562-0497.

Printed in China
13 14 15 16 17 18 LEO 10 9 8 7 6 5 4 3

Editorial Development: Mary Richards Beaumont
Art Direction and Design: Lisa Wilber
Production: Tami Kepler, Sarah Boecher,
Jeannette Bailey, Judith Lary

Illustrations: Julia Bereciartu

Stuff to keep

The best stuff about my family

Big Stuff that's happened to me this year

at home:

at school:

Starting highschool

in my activities:

Other big stuff

Stuff that makes me smile

Stuff I can do that others can't

New foods I've tried

☐ liked it .... ☐ didn't like it

☐ liked it .... ☐ didn't like it

☐ liked it .... ☐ didn't like it

☐ liked it .... ☐ didn't like it

☐ liked it .... ☐ didn't like it

☐ liked it .... ☐ didn't like it

☐ liked it .... ☐ didn't like it

☐ liked it .... ☐ didn't like it

☐ liked it .... ☐ didn't like it

☐ liked it .... ☐ didn't like it

☐ liked it .... ☐ didn't like it

☐ liked it .... ☐ didn't like it

Foods I love

The best stuff to do on weekends

Stuff I do when I'm really, really bored

Stuff on the shelves in my room

Posters and pictures on my walls

My stuffed animals

names	types

Fun and creative ideas for cleaning your room **fast:**

Cleanup Challenge

Set a timer for 15 minutes. Race to put things where they belong before the timer dings.

Shoot It!

Play hoops with your dirty laundry or crumpled notepaper. Where do you have to stand in your room to make a three-point shot?

Store Chore

Pretend that your room is a fancy boutique. Arrange everything nicely so that your customers will want to come back.

Host with the Most

Imagine that you're hosting a home improvement show. Describe to your audience what you're doing and why.

Games and toys I love

Outfits I love

Prety Dresses

Sefuke (uniforms)
fairy Kei

Movies I love   Favorite character

Scott Pilgrem vs the world → Scott

TV shows I love   Favorite character

Doctor who   Rose & Doctor

Books I love

_____

_____

_____

_____

_____

_____

_____

_____

_____

_____

Video games and online games I love

High scores

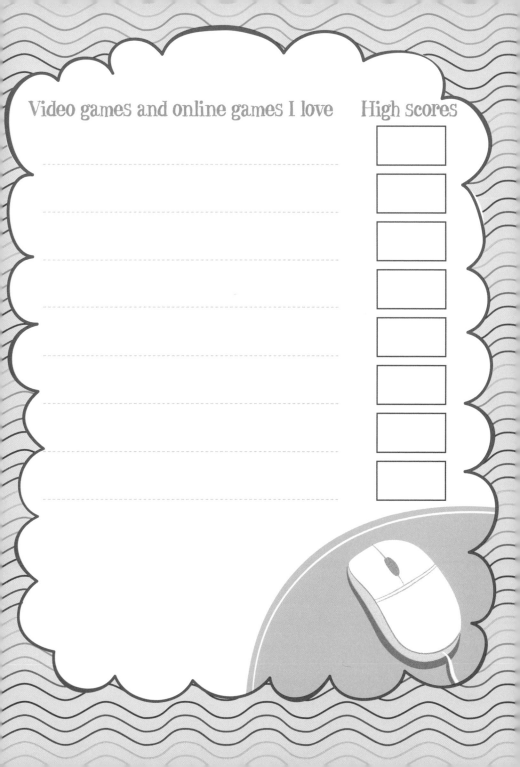

Web sites I love

Tumblr , Pintrest , Google

Funniest stuff I've seen online

Songs I love

Songs that make me want to dance

Singers and bands I love

House rules I'd change
and what I'd change them to

Rule: ....

New rule: ....

Rule: ....

New rule: ....

Rule: ....

New rule: ....

Rule: ....

New rule: ....

Rule: ....

New rule: ....

The stuff that's most important in my life

Friends

My closest friends

Camryn, Ryan, Hailey

Of everyone in this group (including me!), which one is

the best listener? _____

the best advice-giver? _____

the friend who makes me laugh the most? _____

the friend I'd ask for homework help? _____

the one most likely to be a secret superhero? _____

the one most likely to become a millionaire? _____

the one most likely to become famous? _____

the one most likely to invent something? _____

the one most likely to be on TV? _____

the one most likely to become a pro athlete? _____

the one most likely to drive a convertible? _____

the one most likely to go skydiving? _____

the one most likely to live on a farm? _____

the one most likely to travel all over the world? _____

Stuff we do for fun

Slang words we use

Funny stuff that's happened to us

Strange stuff that's happened to us

Important stuff my friends and I agree on

Silly stuff my friends and I agree on

Important stuff my friends and I argue about

Silly stuff my friends and I argue about

School

Classes I'm taking

My teachers

Stuff in my locker (or backpack or desk)

My favorite stuff to
eat for lunch at school

My least favorite stuff to eat for lunch at school

People I sit with at lunch

People I hang out with at recess

The best stuff to do at recess

Go, Blob

Get a bunch of people together and form two circles, one inside the other. Link arms with the people next to you, and move in close. The trick is to move the entire group, as one blob, around the playground. No need to go quickly—just shout out where you think the blob should go next. Invite others to join the blob as you pass them.

Rainbow Tag

Choose a home base. One player is It. The other players are the Rainbow. Each person thinks of a color to be—without saying her color out loud. The person who is It calls out a color. When a player's color is called, she runs for the base and It tries to catch her. If she reaches the base without getting tagged, she chooses another color and rejoins the Rainbow. If she is caught, she's out.

Recess Race

Decide on an obstacle course and see how quickly you can get through it. Go across the monkey bars, run to the swings and pump your legs back and forth 20 times, run up the stairs to the slide, go down the slide, and do 20 jumping jacks. Then have other people do the course. Who can complete it fastest?

Wacky Relay

Divide into teams. Decide which wacky way the runners will race, such as "run in baby steps" or "wave your arms in the air." On "go," the first runners in each team take off in the chosen wacky way, race to a chosen spot, turn around, and come back. They slap hands with the next runners, who will take off in the same wacky way. The first team done wins!

Field trips I've taken

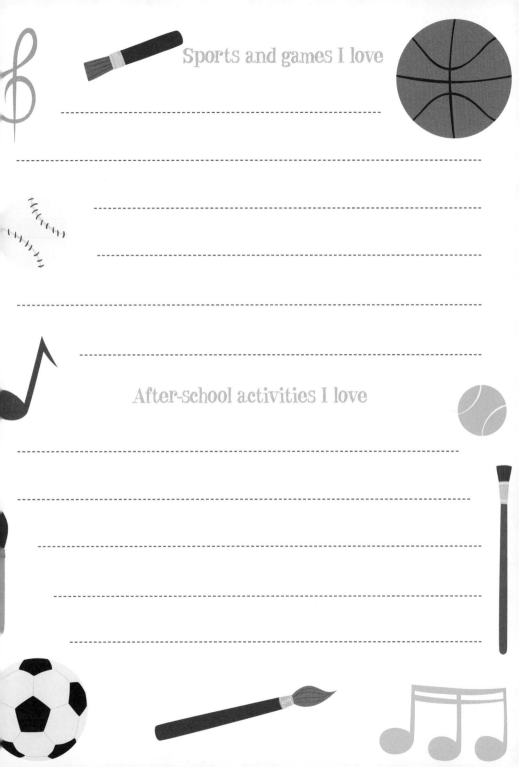

Sports and games I love

After-school activities I love

Really hard stuff I learned to do this year

New words I've learned and what they mean

Awards I've earned

World

Stuff I'd like to change about the world

Stuff I saw on TV that I'll always remember

Faraway places I've visited

Places I've visited near home

Places I'd love to visit

Bumper stickers I like

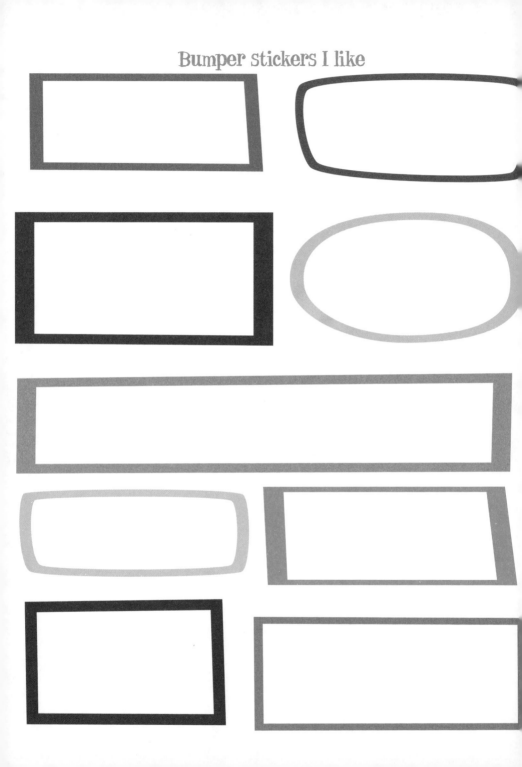

Animals I've seen

Flowers I know the names of

Trees I know the names of

Bugs I've seen

Fun

Things that would be in my
dream bedroom (check them!)

- ☐ a trampoline
- ☑ a hot tub
- ☐ a ballet barre
- ☐ a closet that would tell me what to wear
- ☐ a basketball hoop
- ☑ a library corner filled with books

☑ a wall-sized TV

☑ a fish aquarium I could swim in *without the fish*

☑ a hammock

☑ an ice cream sundae bar

☑ a skee-ball machine

☐ a tree that could grow up through the ceiling

☑ a slide that would take me to the kitchen

☐ a climbing wall

Stuff I'd do if I were trapped
overnight in school

Stuff I'd do if I were trapped overnight in a theme park

Stuff I'd do if I were trapped
overnight in a mall

Stuff I'd do if I were trapped overnight in a sports stadium

How I'd spend $1 million on myself

How I'd spend $1 million to help others

Places I'd go if I could fly

Stuff I'd do if I were invisible

Future

Qualities I want to have (circle them!)

active

ambitious

artistic

athletic

bold

brave

calm

carefree

caring

cheerful

competitive

confident

creative

curious

daring

determined

dramatic

easygoing

energetic

enthusiastic

expressive

friendly

funny

giving

good-natured

goofy

happy

hardworking

helpful

honest

imaginative

independent

intense

interesting

joking

kind

laid-back

laughing

loving

loyal

musical

nice

observant

organized

outdoorsy

outgoing

patient

proud

quiet

resourceful

respectful

responsible

sensitive

smart

strong

stylish

sweet

talkative

thoughtful

trustworthy

Names I'd give a pet dog

Names I'd give a pet cat

Names I'd give a pet fish

Names I'd give a pet bird

Names I'd give a pet _____

Names I'd give a girl child

Names I'd give a boy child

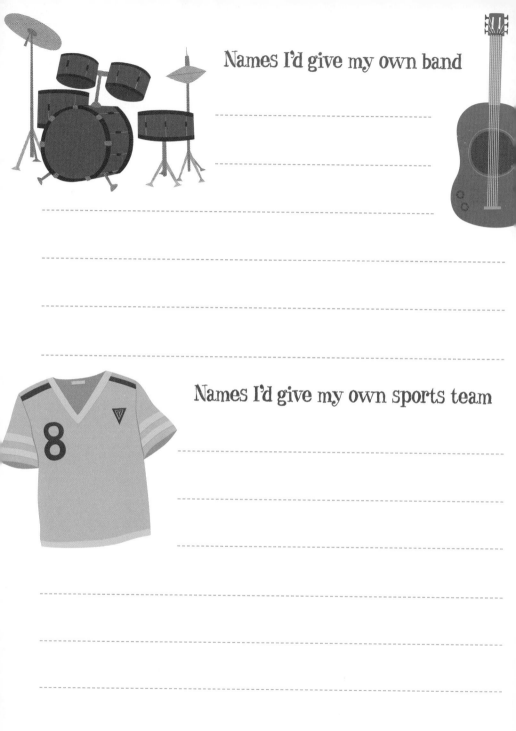

Names I'd give my own band

Names I'd give my own sports team

Names I'd give my own restaurant

Names I'd give my own bakery

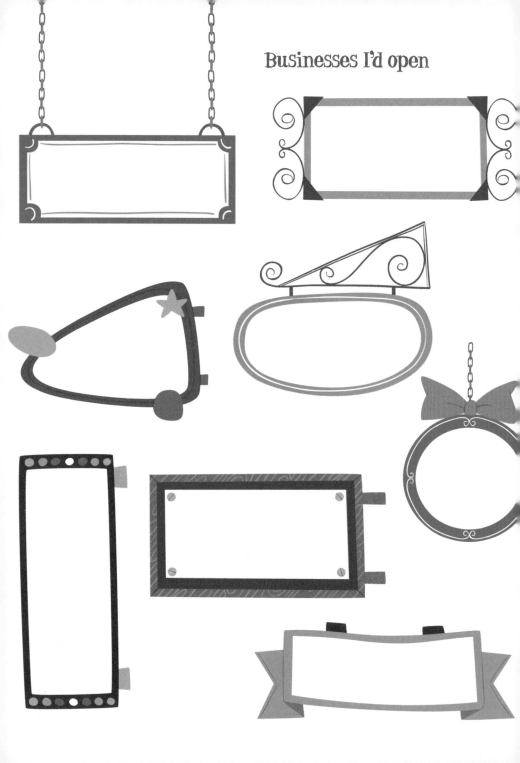

Businesses I'd open

Stuff I wish I knew how to do

Ways to get better at anything

Warm up

Athletes stretch their muscles.
Musicians warm up their fingers.
Singers tune their voices. Ease into
practice with gentle exercises to get
your mind and body in the zone.

What do you know?

Start with what you do well to gain
confidence, and pump yourself up
to work on more challenging things later.

Drill a skill

Pick one skill that you want to get better
at, and do it over and over—and over again!
You'll train your brain, and before you
know it, the skill will seem easier.

End strong

Create a traditional way to end each practice, such as recording your progress or high-fiving your teammates. The point is to finish on a high note.

Set a routine

Set aside time each week to practice. The more you stick to a schedule, the easier it will be to fit practice into your busy life.

Remember this

Does practice make perfect? Nah. Nobody is perfect all the time—not even the pros. But practicing will make you better. It just will.

Goals I have for when I get older

Wishes I want to come true

Share!

How well do you and your friends know one another? Use these tear-out lists to find out! Choose a list topic from the book, and fill in the list as you think your friend would answer. Have her do the same for you. Comparing the lists will help you know each other better.

List

List

List

List

List

List

List

List

List

List

List

List

List

List

List

List

Stuff we'd love to get from you

☆ a letter that shares your favorite list
☆ your great ideas for new lists

Send your stuff to

Lists! Editor
American Girl
8400 Fairway Place
Middleton, WI 53562

Here are some other American Girl books you might like:

☐ I read it.

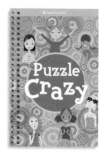

☐ I read it.

☐ I read it.

☐ I read it.

Stars!

Use these stickers to mark your very favorite stuff in all your lists—favorite food, favorite band, favorite whatever.